Sports Illustrated
PITCHING

The Sports Illustrated Library

Sports Illustrated
PITCHING

by PAT JORDAN

Illustrations
by Robert Handville

J. B. LIPPINCOTT COMPANY
New York

U.S. Library of Congress Cataloging in Publication Data

Jordan, Pat.
  Sports illustrated pitching.

  (The Sports illustrated library)
  SUMMARY: Discusses the fundamentals of pitching
and pitch variation. Includes routines for warm-ups,
practices, and development.
  1. Pitching (Baseball) [1. Pitching (Baseball)] I. Handville, Robert. II. Title.
GV871.J67   796.357′22   76–43003
ISBN–0–397–01123–7
ISBN–0–397–01122–9 (pbk.)

Photographs from *Sports Illustrated*, © Time Inc.
Cover and page 14: John Iacona
Pages 8 and 95: Heinz Kluetmeier
Page 56: John Zimmerman
Page 88: Neil Leifer

Photograph on page 92: Fred Kaplan/Black Star

Contents

Sports Illustrated
PITCHING

Introduction

NOT EVERY YOUTH can become a Sandy Koufax or a Tom Seaver, but every youth can become a pitcher, a modestly successful one at that. It is the difference between a craftsman and an artist; the former can be taught and the latter requires a special gift. To be a great pitcher, like Seaver, one must have a superior arm and a great fastball, but there have been numerous successful pitchers—Whitey Ford, for example—who have been able to compensate for a modest fastball by developing a keen pitcher's intelligence, a smooth, deceptive delivery, pinpoint control, and a wide assortment of off-speed and breaking pitches. All of these attributes can be taught to any modestly talented, willing, and intelligent youth. You *can* learn how to pitch! Your success might be limited to high-school baseball or maybe to Babe Ruth and American Legion baseball. Perhaps even collegiate baseball, or baseball as advanced as the minor leagues. But still, with practice you will have experienced not only some of the joys of pitching but—even better—of pitching right.

9

Young pitchers, especially preteens, should concentrate on three aspects of their craft. First and most importantly, they should learn to throw the ball with a natural and proper motion. This includes both their arm motion and their pitching delivery (pump, kick, follow-through, and so forth). A pitcher's motion is like the foundation of an elaborately constructed mansion. No matter how expensive the interior paneling may be, that mansion will be a failure if its foundation is flawed. The same with a pitcher's motion. It is what leads him to his best fastball, sharpest curve, and finest control. It is the foundation on which every single aspect of his craft rests. No matter how much a pitcher sweats and strains, he will never develop his best fastball unless he first develops his proper motion.

Second, as a young pitcher you should try to develop strength in your arm so that you can throw your best and most natural fastball. You should, as quickly as possible, reach the limits of your natural talent. The secret of pitching is to develop a good fastball first, and only later, for the times when the fastball will be insufficient to develop other, less natural pitches like the curveball to compensate. In other words, a young pitcher should throw only fastballs until his teenage years. At that point he can begin work on other pitches.

There are two dangers to a young pitcher in throwing curveballs too soon: it could damage his arm, or it could take away speed from his developing fastball. Damage can occur when the pitcher begins throwing a curveball with an incorrect motion, an easy habit to fall into when young. On the other hand, a properly thrown curveball puts *less* strain on a pitcher's arm than a properly thrown fastball, since a curveball motion is more natural than a fastball motion. And since there is less strain, the arm will remain weaker, more undeveloped than if the pitcher were throwing mostly fastballs.

The third basic of pitching is control. While the young pitcher is developing his motion and speed, he should simultaneously be developing his control—i.e., his ability to throw the ball over any part of the plate he wants. All three basics are intertwined so that the development of any one leads to the advancement of the others. The better you throw the ball, the faster will be your pitch and the easier your control.

If there is a fourth basic to pitching, it is a basic so intangible that it cannot really be taught. With time and pitching experience, you should develop what is commonly called "savvy," which is really a pitcher's intelligence. Some say it is instinct. Others claim that savvy can be learned, that all it requires is a modestly intelligent, willing, and attentive mind. Whichever is true, only time will tell, and the best you can do is to remain mentally alert and receptive to experience whenever you are on the mound. For example, when a batter takes such a hard swing at your pitch that he pulls your best fastball into foul territory, your intelligence should tell you that he will miss a slower pitch—so throw one.

The only way to develop all three (or four) basics of pitching is by pitching. There are no drills or calisthenics that can develop these basics as quickly, as properly, and as naturally as the simple act of pitching a baseball. However, you cannot pitch a game every day, nor can you simply throw a ball every day. The strain on your arm will be too great. At most, a young pitcher should pitch no more than two games a week, and should throw a baseball (i.e., warm-up and/or game) no more than four times a week. The ideal throwing schedule is to warm up two days before you pitch in a game, and then to warm up two days after. In between these bouts of throwing, you should not put any strain on your arm. This does not mean you can't "soft-toss" a leisurely game of catch, but even in this soft-tossing, you should concentrate on your craft of throwing a ball, no matter how easily, with the proper motion. A pitcher should always throw like a pitcher even when playing catch with an infielder. His every baseball moment should be designed to

11

practice his natural pitching delivery until it no longer becomes a thing learned, but simply a natural extension of himself, like walking.

Warming up, an art in itself, can determine a pitcher's success or lack of it in any given game. The proper way to warm up before a game is to begin by taking a light run around the park to loosen your muscles and get the adrenaline flowing; then, after a light set of calisthenics (i.e., touching toes, jumping jacks, sit-ups), you should start throwing to the catcher from a distance of, say, 45 feet—assuming you intend to pitch from the regulation major-league distance of 60 feet 6 inches. This "short throwing" is more for psychological ease than anything else, and you should advance to the regulation distance as quickly as possible. On each successive pitch you should extend your arm farther. A sustained period of soft lobs accomplishes nothing. Conversely, throwing your best fastball before you are sufficiently warmed up can damage your arm. Only after you have advanced to your best fastball and have thrown about eight of them should you begin lofting slow curveballs until, again, you are throwing your hardest curveball.

At this point the pitcher should begin to mix up his pitches, fastball, curveball, fastball, and so forth, just as he would in a game. He should finish his warm-ups from between ten to fifteen minutes after he has started throwing. To throw longer than fifteen minutes will tire a pitcher out before he even takes the mound, and to throw less will risk the possibility of injuring an insufficiently loosened-up arm.

On off days when a pitcher is not throwing—even on days when he will merely warm up—he should undergo a routine of calisthenics and running designed both to loosen the muscles in his limbs, back, and shoulders and to strengthen the muscles in his legs. A pitcher's legs are almost as important to his pitching as is his arm. They must sustain the strenuous pushing off the rubber for more than one hundred pitches a game.

Throwing a baseball is a stretching, reaching motion that requires elastic, loose muscles, and calisthenics should include a variety of muscle-stretching and loosening routines. Sit-ups, toe touching, jumping jacks, and so forth are excellent for this purpose. On the other hand, routines that tighten and constrict a pitcher's muscles, such as pushups and weight lifting, are less helpful and sometimes even harmful—although in some isolated cases, weight lifting can be beneficial. If a pitcher's arm is basically weak or if he is recovering from a sore arm, then weight lifting can help. But in general, a young pitcher should avoid weight lifting until well into his teens, when he will better know whether or not he will need its special benefits.

For running exercises, you will get more benefit from short, all-out sprints than you will from leisurely jogging. Jogging will loosen up a pitcher's legs, but short sprints will develop leg power which can sustain the long ardor of a game. A good sprinting routine is to run full speed for 100 yards, walk 50 yards, and so on for about ten to twenty sprints a day. But remember, running and calisthenics are merely peripheral aids to throwing a baseball. No amount of either can be anywhere near as beneficial as the simple act of throwing. The only way anyone can become a pitcher is to pitch.

1
The Motion

ALL SUCCESSFUL PITCHERS succeed for the same reason. They throw the ball with a smooth and classically correct motion. Such a motion is the common denominator which separates Tom Seaver, Catfish Hunter, Sandy Koufax, and Warren Spahn from their less successful brethren. Granted, the motions of each of these great pitchers contain certain idiosyncrasies, but they all contain the same basic pitching mechanics, all part of a carefully constructed routine whose purpose is to produce the maximum effort. A pitcher's motion is like the workings of an auto engine. Both contain a dozen revolving and pumping parts, all of which help build up power and rhythm that propel the ball—or the engine— in a particular direction at a particular speed. A proper pitching motion will help the pitcher throw the ball with his maximum strength, will help him throw the ball in a desired direction, will put the least amount of strain on his arm, a fragile limb never designed for the steady throwing of a baseball, and finally, it will help him deceive his opponent, the batter.

15

Let me illustrate and define proper pitching mechanics. Our subject pitcher will be a right-handed thrower, although the same rules will apply equally (although conversely) to left-handed throwers.

STANCE

The purpose of a proper stance on the rubber is to give the pitcher correct balance before he begins his elaborate motion, so as to make sure his weight is properly distributed in preparation for the shifting back and forth which occurs throughout a pitcher's delivery.

With no runners on base, the pitcher takes his sign from the catcher with his right foot bisecting the rubber and pointing toward the catcher. His left foot should be a few inches behind and to the left of his right foot (Diagram 1).

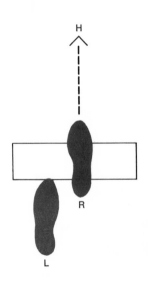

**Diagram 1. The Stance:
Foot Position**

The left leg should be slightly flexed so that most of the pitcher's weight is forward on his right leg, as if he is already about to explode toward the batter (Figure 1). The pitcher can take his sign in either of two ways: with his glove hand at his side and his ball hand behind his back, or else with the ball hand and glove hand joined in front at his waist as if in prayer. The purpose of both positions is to conceal the pitcher's grip on the ball so that the batter will not be able to tell what kind of pitch will be coming.

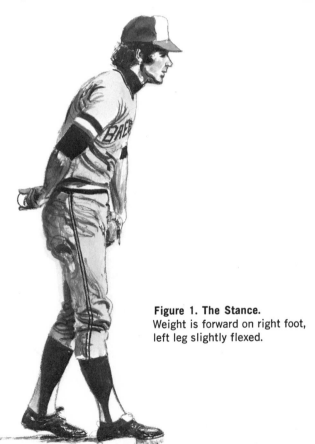

Figure 1. The Stance.
Weight is forward on right foot, left leg slightly flexed.

PUMP

The pitcher's pump helps to build the proper rhythm from which most good pitchers obtain much of their power. It also helps to position the pitcher's foot securely against

Figure 2. The Pump.

A. As hands rise, weight shifts back onto left leg.

B. Forward motion begins as right foot turns parallel to rubber.

the rubber so that he can push off with his maximum force toward the plate.

The pitcher begins his motion with both hands joined at his waist. As both joined hands rise in front of his eyes, his weight shifts from his right foot back to his left foot so that he appears to be leaning back away from the batter (Figure 2A). When his hands are almost fully extended (and still joined) above his head, almost all his weight will be resting on his still flexed left leg, while his right foot is only lightly touching the rubber. In this position the pitcher slides his right foot off the rubber by turning it parallel to the rubber—toe facing third base—and then sliding it forward into the indentation in the dirt that is always found next to a pitching rubber on a mound (Figure 2B). His position now resembles that of a fencer about to spring forward on the attack.

KICK

The purpose of the kick is to shift the weight backward toward second base, in such a way that the pitcher still retains his balance but also builds up a kind of rocking back-and-forth rhythm that eventually will evolve into a physical explosion toward the plate.

The pitcher's weight now moves forward onto his right foot, and as it does, his left foot leaves the ground. His body swivels from left to right toward third base, his left leg rising as he swivels, until he has turned himself completely sideways to the batter. At this point he resembles a crane standing on one leg in a swamp (Figure 3). All his weight is now on his right foot. His left leg is raised

19

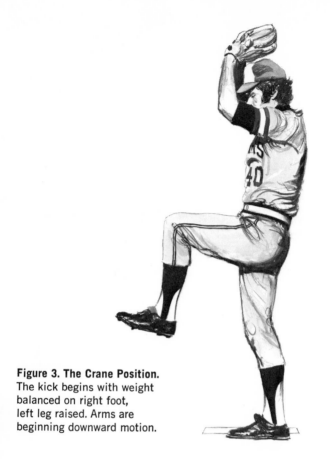

Figure 3. The Crane Position.
The kick begins with weight
balanced on right foot,
left leg raised. Arms are
beginning downward motion.

and bent at a level with his waist. His hands above his
head are just beginning their descent toward his bent left
leg. If properly executed this position can be held indefi-
nitely in a state of perfect balance. If at this point a pitcher
finds himself falling forward toward third base (Figure
4A), then his weight is not perpendicular to the rubber as
it should be. The same is true if he finds himself falling
backward toward first base (Figure 4B). Meanwhile, his
hands have simultaneously moved down toward his bent

Figure 4. Improper balance.

A. Weight too far forward

B. Weight too far back

leg. Just before they touch the raised knee, the two hands separate. The glove hand falls on the home-plate side of the raised knee and the ball hand falls on the second-base side of the knee and begins to move back and down toward second base. It is important for the pitcher's ball hand to move directly toward second base. If it swings back too far toward first base, the pitcher will be in a "locked" position (Figure 5), and his body rhythm will be out of sync, so that

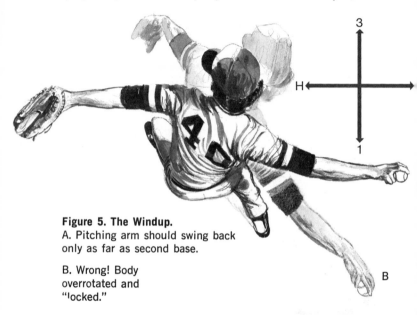

Figure 5. The Windup.
A. Pitching arm should swing back only as far as second base.

B. Wrong! Body overrotated and "locked."

when his body moves forward toward the plate, his arm, instead of moving toward the plate simultaneously, will follow much later.

Still standing like a crane, the pitcher's weight now shifts slightly back toward second base, as if his ball hand is trying to reach back to touch the base. Again, if the pitcher reaches too far back he will lose his balance—so essential to good pitching. His hips should be tilted in such a way that his left hip facing the plate is higher than his right hip facing second base (Figure 6). Next, the pitcher begins his

2nd

Figure 6. Hip Tilt.
The kickout begins from a balanced position, hips tilted toward
second, pitching arm reaching down and back toward second base.

spring forward toward the batter. His arm and all his weight explode simultaneously toward the batter. His raised left leg kicks out at a point halfway between home plate and third base and then swings from right to left toward the plate (Figures 7A, 7B, 7C). His hips swivel from right to left, and as his left leg pulls the pitcher's body toward the plate, his right foot, firmly placed against the rubber, simultaneously pushes off the rubber toward the plate. Much of

Figure 7. The Kick

B. Momentum is developed as the body rotates, following the left leg.

A. The left leg kicks out and swings forward toward home.

C. As the left foot lands in the stride position, it pulls the body forward, which, with the simultaneous pushing off the rubber with the right foot, produces much of the pitcher's power.

a pitcher's power comes from the combined force of the left leg's kick toward the plate and the right leg's thrust off the rubber. This power catapults his entire body toward the batter and, almost as his arm, is responsible for the speed of his fastball. It is for this most important push that great pitchers like Tom Seaver work so hard at strengthening their calves and thighs.

STRIDE

As much as any part of his delivery, a pitcher's stride will determine where the ball will be thrown. The length and position of that stride will directly influence a pitcher's control and is often the first part of a pitcher's motion he must alter in order to change the direction of his pitches.

As the left leg is swinging from third base toward the plate, the pitcher's arm is simultaneously moving forward (with the rest of his body) from second base. When the pitcher's left foot comes down on the dirt, his right arm should be passing alongside of his head (Figure 8). At this

Figure 8. The Stride.
In the full-stride position
the legs are far apart, the upper body
has lunged forward, and the
throwing arm is passing the head.

point the pitcher's legs are spread about as far apart as possible. He is very low to the ground. All his weight from the waist up is lunging forward toward the batter. His left leg is bent, and his left foot is planted firmly in the dirt for balance and pulling power; it literally grips the dirt like a claw and pulls the pitcher forward. His right leg is stretched backward in an almost direct line with the rest of his body—his right foot still in contact with the rubber.

As the pitcher releases the ball at a point about 12 inches in front of his head, his right foot leaves the rubber and his right leg swings up—about as high as his waist (Figure 9)—before it comes down toward the plate. Even after he has released the ball, the pitcher's arm still continues its flight toward the plate in conjunction with his swinging right leg. When the right leg is finally down and the right foot touches the dirt, it should touch at a point parallel to or a few inches ahead of the left foot, with the feet from 18 to 24 inches apart.

Figure 9. The Release.
As the ball is released, the right leg leaves the rubber, swinging up and forward. The throwing arm continues its proper motion toward the plate.

FOLLOW-THROUGH

Like the stride, the follow-through will help determine a pitcher's control and, if properly executed, will give a bit of additional speed to his pitch by carrying him forward toward the batter. It will also give the pitcher the proper balance needed to field balls hit back through the mound.

Figure 10. Proper Follow-Through.
Arm travels forward and down across the chest, coming to rest near the left ankle. Body is bent over, with weight on left leg.
Face is down until follow-through is complete.

WEIGHT

The pitcher's arm should continue forward, passing in front of his chest and down, until it comes to rest at a point about 2 inches to the left of his left ankle (Figure 10). The pitcher is now bent well over, his face staring at the ground, with all the weight of his body centered on his left leg and foot. The right foot should be merely touching the ground lightly for balance—to keep the pitcher from falling over. From their original starting position on the rubber, the pitcher's feet should be in the following position (Diagram 2): his left foot should be about 4 feet

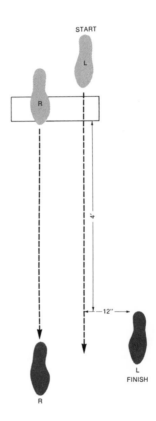

Diagram 2.
The Follow-Through:
Correct Foot Position

in front of the rubber (depending on the length of the pitcher's stride and of his legs) and about 12 inches to the left of its starting point. His right foot should also be 4 feet in front of its starting point; however, it should be straight ahead. In other words, the pitcher's legs are now spread apart considerably more than when he began his motion on the rubber. This is called "opening up," and it greatly affects a pitcher's speed and control.

COMMON ERRORS

What passes for pitching genius—and what often separates good pitchers from great pitchers—is a pitcher's ability to pick up his own pitching errors either during or immediately after he has thrown a pitch. Tom Seaver, for example, is his own best coach. He can tell immediately after he has thrown a high curveball, for instance, what he has done wrong in his motion to make that curveball go high, and then what he should do to correct the error. And, of course, he has the physical and mental talent to correct it on his next pitch. However, the rest of us mortals may not be so gifted. The best we can hope for is to have an intelligent pitching coach who will help us spot such errors in our delivery, which we, caught up in the moment, cannot see. Pitching errors occur generally when a pitcher's concentration slips and he forgets to execute part of his motion properly, when he is physically weak or tired, or when his motion is flawed or insufficiently developed. The best way to avoid errors in pitching is by correcting them while pitching or warming up. No amount of "trick drills" will help a pitcher perfect his motion or break bad habits better than the simple act of pitching.

One of the most common errors made by young pitchers is called "rushing." This occurs when the pitcher should be in the crane position (shown in Figure 3) facing third base, but has swung his left leg too far back toward short-

30

stop, which in turn has pulled his right arm too far toward first base instead of back toward second base. At this point a pitcher has almost turned his back on the batter. When the pitcher begins to move forward in this rushing position, two things happen that will affect his speed and control. First, his legs and body will be moving ahead of his arm, and second, his rhythm will be out of sync. His body weight will not be helping his arm speed but will be so far ahead of it that he is just throwing or flinging the ball with his arm without benefit of his body motion. Usually his left foot will land on the ground before his right arm passes alongside of his head, rather than at the same moment (Figure 11). With his rhythm spent, his right arm will swing forward all by itself, greatly lessening the speed of the pitch.

Figure 11. Rushing.
Power is lost when body weight and motion get too far ahead of throwing arm.

Another error common among young pitchers is failing to open up—that is, the pitcher does not pull his left leg far enough to the left during his stride and follow-through. This stems from a lazy or weak left leg. The left foot, instead of landing 12 inches or so to the left of its starting point, lands in a direct line with or maybe even to the right of its starting point (Diagram 3). This is too soon, with the result that the arm and body movements are out of sync. Again, the body rhythm has been spent before the release, and a pitcher is just throwing with his arm. Also, in an unopened position the pitcher's weight will not be resting solely on his left foot but will be equally divided between his right and left foot. This forces his body to lunge to the right of the plate. The pitcher's arm, instead of crossing in front of his chest and down toward his left ankle, will shoot out straight, and the ball will travel high and inside without good speed. To find out if you are not opening up enough, merely remain in your follow-through for a second. If your weight is too heavily on your right foot and your arm finishes up alongside of your right foot

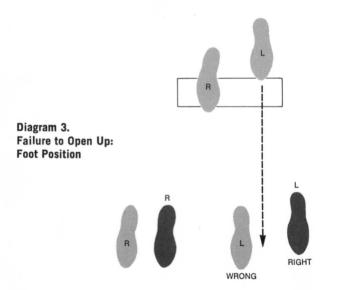

**Diagram 3.
Failure to Open Up:
Foot Position**

instead of your left, you definitely have not opened up enough (Figure 12).

Still another error of young pitchers is taking too short a stride. The stride should be as long as is comfortably possible while still retaining good balance. Too short a stride will cause the ball to be released early, resulting in a high pitch. Too long a stride will result in an exceptionally low pitch—always better than a higher one. A pitcher has only to adjust his stride a bit after each pitch to raise or lower his fastball. If he follows through too far to his left, the ball will be too far off the left-hand corner of the plate; too far to the right and the pitch will be too far off the right-hand corner. A simple adjustment in his follow-through should correct either problem.

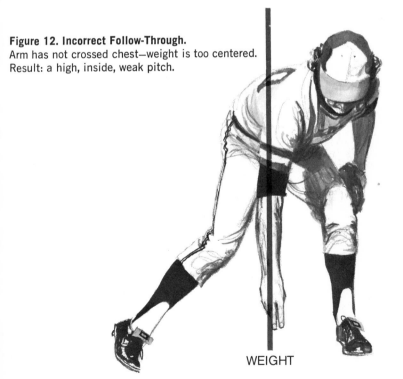

Figure 12. Incorrect Follow-Through.
Arm has not crossed chest—weight is too centered.
Result: a high, inside, weak pitch.

WEIGHT

Figure 13. The Total Motion.
It is all here: proper stance, kick, stride, release,
and follow-through, each element essential to a
proper motion. The mechanics of the motion are
all-important and should constantly be practiced
and refined.

STRETCH MOTION

With a runner on first base, the pitcher takes his sign standing sideways to the batter, his right foot already parallel to the rubber. His left foot should be about 8 inches in front of his right foot and a few inches to the left (Diagram 4). His weight should rest mostly on his slightly flexed right leg, his left leg straight and supporting only a minimum of his weight (Figure 14). In fact, he is almost leaning back toward first base, as if he were going to wheel

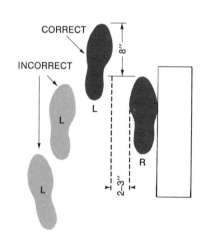

CORRECT

INCORRECT

8"

L

L

R

2–3"

**Diagram 4.
Stretch Foot Position**

at any moment and try to pick the runner off. Now, with his hands joined at his waist, the pitcher is ready to begin his motion. All he has to do is raise his left leg straight up and he will find himself in the perfect crane position (shown in Figure 3). This stretch motion allows him to get into the crane position very quickly, thus foiling a runner who is attempting to steal. The more motion a pitcher takes before he gets into the crane position, the more time a runner has to steal.

Figure 14.
Stretch Position

A common mistake of young pitchers is to take their sign in the stretch position but with their left and right feet either side by side or with the left foot behind the right foot (Diagram 4). In this position, once the pitcher raises his left leg, he also has to swing it toward third base before swinging it back toward the plate, losing valuable time during which the runner can steal. Some pitchers claim that positioning their left foot more toward first base makes it easier for them to wheel and throw over to first. However, since a pitcher's primary concern is holding a runner on the

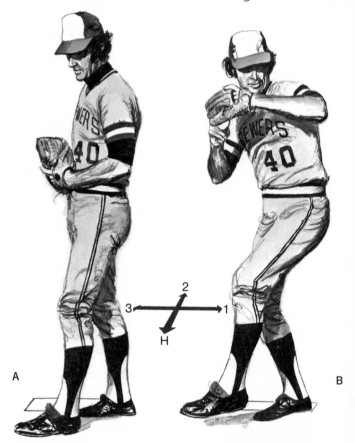

Figure 15. Pickoff, First Base

base, not to pick him off—a rare occurrence—he should use the stretch position in Diagram 4. From this position he can deliver the ball to the plate quicker than from any other position and can allow a runner the least time to take off.

When a pitcher does throw to first, he simply pivots on his right foot (touching the rubber) and wheels his left foot around from third base to first base (Figures 15A, 15B, 15C). In attempting a pickoff at second base, he makes the same movements, only his left foot swings all the way

C

around from third base, past home plate and first base to second base (Figures 16A, 16B, 16C, 16D). It's almost as if he were performing a dancer's pirouette. In a pickoff attempt at third (which is identical to that of a left-handed

A   B

Figure 16. Pickoff, Second Base

pitcher attempting to pickoff a runner at first), the right-handed pitcher merely raises his left leg until he is in the crane position and then, instead of kicking toward third base and swinging his leg around toward home plate, he

C

Figure 17. Pickoff, Third Base

kicks toward third base, then throws straight to the bag (Figures 17A, 17B, 17C). This is the easiest pickoff motion of all.

ARM MOTION

There are three basic arm motions: overhand, three-quarters overhand, and sidearm. A pitcher should throw

42

B

A

with the motion most comfortable to him. He also should stick to one motion and not switch back and forth between, say, sidearm and overhand. True, some pitchers like Juan Marichal have been able to master a variety of arm motions, but they are the exception. If a pitcher throws every pitch —fastball, curveball, change-up—with the same motion, the batter will be more easily deceived. The ball will always come towards him at the same angle, yet will be doing

43

different things each time. This is the height of deception. The secret lies in the appearance of sameness and the reality of change.

Most power pitchers who rely mainly on explosive fastballs throw with either a straight overhand or a three-quarters overhand motion. This motion allows the pitcher to get more of his upper body (upper back, shoulders) into each pitch. Assuming he is in the crane position, to throw

A. Side

Figure 18. Overhand Fastball.
As throwing arm passes head, shoulders are tilted toward first; arm is partially bent.

the ball overhand his arm reaches back and down toward second base almost to the point of touching the ground. When his body and arm begin to move forward, the arm travels forward and up until it rises to a point from 18 to 24 inches above and to the side of his right ear (Figure 18A). His shoulders should be tilted so that his left shoulder is pointing down toward first base and his right shoulder is pointing up toward third base (Figure 18B).

B. Rear

Figure 19. Overhand Fastball:
Incorrect Positions

A. Arm too straight.
Loss of power and speed.

At this point the pitcher's arm is partially bent in a modified L design and not fully extended. If it is straight (Figure 19A), he will lose the whiplike elbow action that gives his fastball much of its speed. His arm will be stiff and he will be flinging the ball mostly with back and

B. Arm overly bent.
Difficult to apply shoulder power.

shoulder power. On the other hand, if his arm is bent too much at the elbow (Figure 19B), he will be slingshotting the ball as a catcher does, using mostly the strength of his forearm and losing much of the shoulder action that gives his fastball speed.

Figure 20. Pushing.
When the elbow gets ahead of the wrist, most shoulder power is lost, resulting in a weak, soft pitch.

Also at this point, the pitcher's arm from elbow to wrist should be vertical. If his elbow is ahead of his wrist (Figure 20), he will merely be pushing the ball toward the plate with his forearm, much in the same manner as unathletic girls throwing a ball. He will lose a lot of the important shoulder action.

Figure 21. Approaching Release.
Wrist is slightly ahead of elbow
as arm passes ear.

Assuming that the pitcher's forearm is now vertical, the elbow even with his right ear, his arm continues its forward and downward motion toward the plate, but the moment the arm passes in front of his head, his wrist begins to move ahead of his elbow (Figure 21), and the arm begins to straighten out until the ball is released—about 15 inches in front of his head. At that point, the arm is almost but not quite straight. It straightens out completely only after the ball has left the hand. Also, at the moment of release the pitcher's wrist snaps forward so that his wrist combines with his forearm, elbow, shoulders, and upper back to propel the ball forward and down (Figure 22). This wrist action puts a great deal of spin on the ball, giving a fastball most of the spinning motion which, cutting through

Figure 22. Wrist Snap.
At the moment of release, the wrist snaps forward.
This puts spin on a fastball and helps transmit the full power of the upper body.

the air currents, makes the ball move in one direction or another. A properly thrown overhand fastball will have an upward-spinning motion, causing the ball to rise.

After the hand has released the ball, the arm continues forward, down, and slightly to the left. It crosses the pitcher's chest and continues down until it comes to rest near the left ankle (as shown in Figure 10). If the arm only goes across the pitcher's chest and not down, he will lose the benefit of all the upper back motion which is propelling the rest of his body. This means that the arm motion will be going one way—right to left—while the body motion is going another—downward. Correct pitching requires all the parts of the body to move simultaneously in the same direction.

Besides generating maximum speed with this overhand motion, the pitcher also gains the advantage of delivering the ball at both a right-to-left and up-to-down angle. Thus the batter has to gauge not only the ball's speed but the various angles of approach. And the more a batter must think before he can tell himself whether or not to swing, the more it is to the pitcher's advantage. The most difficult angle for a batter is an up-to-down one, rather than right-to-left. The obvious reason is that the bat is longer than it is wide. Because a bat is usually about 36 inches long and only about 4 inches wide—only 1 inch of which is true hitting wood—a hitter can more easily reach a right-to-left pitch than he can an up-to-down pitch. Of course, the ideal pitch moves in both directions, compounding the batter's computations.

The three-quarters overhand motion, used so successfully by Tom Seaver, is also an excellent motion for a fastball pitcher. With the pitcher in his stride position, his arm will not be as high over his head as with an overhand delivery, nor will it be as close to the right ear. The elbow will be bent more, so that the arm is in a much tighter L shape than with the overhand motion (Figure 23). The pitcher's shoulders also are less tilted but still not perfectly parallel to the ground. As the pitcher's arm moves forward and releases the ball, it will travel in more of a right-to-left direction than an up-to-down direction. This is the disadvantage of this pitch as compared with a directly overhand delivery. However, the advantage is that it is easier to make a ball "move"—i.e., sink, rise, or tail in to a right-handed batter—than with an overhand delivery, which will generally move in only one direction—up—as it crosses the plate, and then only when a pitcher throws it with great speed. An overhand fastball without great speed is merely a straight pitch and considerably easier to hit than a three-quarters fastball which, though without great speed, has some additional movement on it as it crosses the plate. More on how to make pitches move will be discussed in the next section, "The Pitches."

Figure 23.
Three-Quarters Overhand Motion.
Shoulders are less tilted and throwing arm more bent than in overhand.

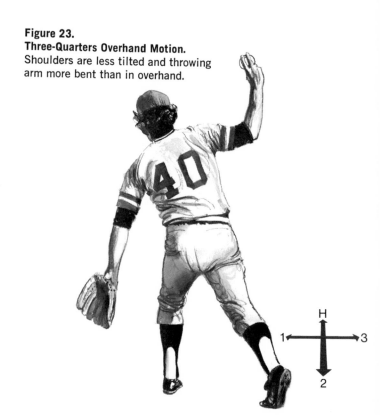

A sidearm pitch will generally have less speed than either a three-quarters or an overhand pitch, because the pitcher will lose much of his back and shoulder action and will be throwing the ball almost entirely with his arm. This pitch also puts a greater strain on a pitcher's arm, particularly the elbow, than either of the other pitches.

To throw a sidearm fastball, the pitcher starts in the crane position; then, when his throwing arm moves back, it rotates more toward first base—right to left—than back and down toward second, as with the other two pitches. His whole arm and body motion is more right to left, with very little up and down. As the pitcher's arm moves toward the plate and passes alongside of his head, the arm is almost perfectly parallel to the ground, with the ball at a level with his right ear (Figure 24). His shoulders also are par-

Figure 24. Sidearm Motion.
Arm is almost parallel to ground, with slight bend; shoulders are level. Power is generated almost solely with a rotational movement.

allel to the ground, with no up-down tilt. His elbow is only slightly bent. When his arm and body swing around from right to left toward the plate, there is practically no downward movement of his arm or body. The ball will approach the plate almost totally in a right-to-left direction (Figure 25), although there will be a slightly downward

Figure 25. Sidearm Pitch: Batter's View

angle—the main disadvantage to this pitch. The advantages are that a sidearm pitch has a great deal of last-minute movement, especially tail and sink. Most sidearm pitchers like Bruce Kison of the Pirates have excellent sinkerballs, which makes them very good relievers, since sinkerballs are generally hit on the ground, helping produce double plays.

As mentioned earlier, a pitcher should find that arm motion which feels most comfortable and stick to it. What is comfortable to Bruce Kison is not necessarily comfortable to Tom Seaver or Ferguson Jenkins. As E. B. White once said about writing, "The style is the man." You cannot go against your grain.

2
The Pitches

FASTBALL

The pitch most thrown in major-league baseball and most often maligned is the fastball. "All big-league hitters supposedly murder fastballs," goes the consensus of professionals. A pitcher can't pitch successfully in the major leagues relying mainly on a fastball, yet more outs are recorded on fastballs every game than on any other single pitch. It is the basic pitch; every other pitch is a variation. Every pitcher throws a fastball whether a knuckleball pitcher or a fastball pitcher, and yet, not every pitcher throws a knuckleball, a slider, or even a curveball. Therefore, it is safe to say that the fastball is the most important pitch in any pitcher's arsenal. If he's basically a fastball pitcher, he needs that pitch for most of his outs, and if he's a breaking-ball pitcher, he needs a fastball to offset his breaking balls. The irony is that most pitchers spend endless hours in the bullpen trying to improve their curveball, slider, and so forth, and generally neglect their fastball, feeling that the pitch is just a natural gift that they can't improve. Wrong! Even their natural limits can be extended. Any pitcher can learn to throw his fastball harder than he ever imagined he could, throw it to the right spot at an appropriate moment, and finally, throw it so that it does not merely approach the plate in a straight line but at the last second takes an additional rise, dip, or tail.

There is only one basic way to grip the ball, whether a

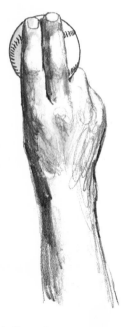
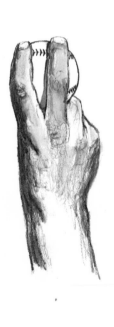

A. Correct   B. Incorrect

Figure 26. The Fastball Grip

pitcher throws his fastball with an overhand, three-quarters or sidearm motion. It is gripped with the first two fingers of his hand cutting directly across the center of the ball (Figure 26A). Those fingers should be close together, not spread apart (Figure 26B). The pressure points on the ball should be the center, meaty part of those two fingertips, not the extreme tips (Figure 26C). The ball should not be gripped tightly, jammed against the inside of the pitcher's hand (Figure 26D), but should be held with a slight air space between the ball and the hand (Figure 26C). The thumb grips the underside of the ball as another

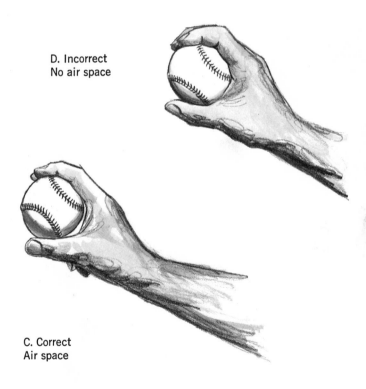

D. Incorrect
No air space

C. Correct
Air space

pressure point, but the extreme tip of the thumb should not press on the ball; the pressure should be on that meaty part of the thumb closer to the knuckle (Figure 27). The third pressure point is located on the side of the ball where the pitcher's third finger is knuckled under. The pressure is directly against the knuckle of that third finger. To repeat, the ball should not be jammed tightly into the pitcher's hand, but should be held with a slight air space be-

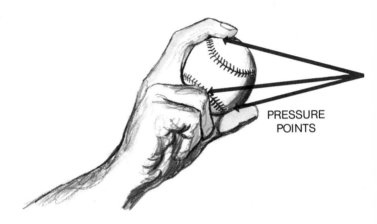

PRESSURE
POINTS

Figure 27. Fastball Pressure Points

tween the ball and his inner palm. Also, the fingers should not be wrapped tightly around the ball, merely firmly. The only tight pressure on the ball should be at the three pressure points. It is this pressure which gives the fastball its excessive spinning motion at the point of release. A ball held tightly all over will not spin as much as one held tightly only at the pressure points.

The basic fastball is held with the first two fingers bisecting the ball's seams on top (Figure 28A) and the thumb bisecting the seam on the bottom (Figure 28B). The pressure points in both places are directly on the seams, which operate almost like handles to give the pitcher

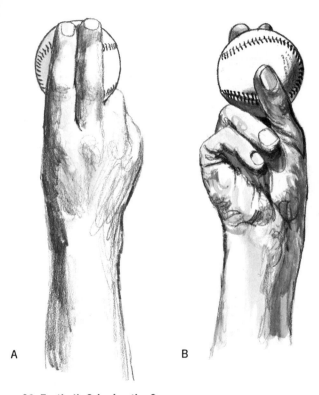

A   B

Figure 28. Fastball: Gripping the Seams.
Pressure points are on the seams: the first two fingers cross the top seam (A): the thumb bisects the bottom seam (B).

a firm grip on the ball. When the pitch. is thrown, the pitcher's top two fingers pull down on the top seam, directly cutting through the heart of the ball (Figure 29) and causing the ball to spin upward. At the same moment,

61

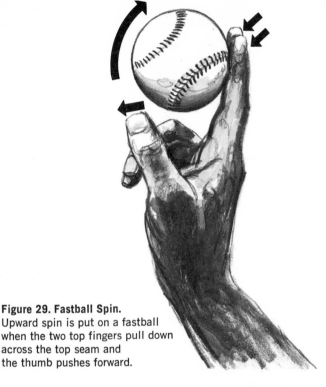

Figure 29. Fastball Spin.
Upward spin is put on a fastball
when the two top fingers pull down
across the top seam and
the thumb pushes forward.

the pitcher's thumb is pushing forward on the other seam, which accelerates the spin. This double action against the seams, by producing an upward spin at maximum speed, makes the ball look smaller as it approaches the batter— an optical illusion that serves to a pitcher's advantage. A slower-spinning ball looks large and easy to hit, with its red seams more visible to the batter, whereas a fast-spinning ball becomes merely a small white blur with no sharply defined edges or seams. The fast spinning also has the advantage of giving the ball a certain last-second movement as it reaches the plate.

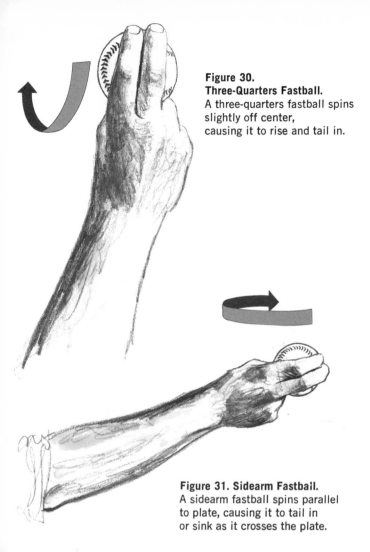

Figure 30.
Three-Quarters Fastball.
A three-quarters fastball spins
slightly off center,
causing it to rise and tail in.

Figure 31. Sidearm Fastball.
A sidearm fastball spins parallel
to plate, causing it to tail in
or sink as it crosses the plate.

An overhand fastball should cross the plate with a rising motion, (Figure 32, A). A three-quarters fastball should be spinning up and slightly off center (Figure 30), crossing the plate both rising and tailing in to a right-handed hitter (Figure 32, B). And a sidearm fastball should be spinning directly parallel to the ground (Figure 31).

**Figure 32. Different Fastballs:
Right-Handed Batter's View**

An overhand fastball rises as it crosses the plate
(A): a three-quarters fastball rises and tails in (B).

Some pitchers try to make their fastballs "move" by artificial means. They deliberately cut through the ball off center so that the ball will spin off center and move in a desired direction. For example, when a pitcher throwing overhand or three-quarters tries to make a ball move artificially, he will cut down through and slightly to the left of the ball, his first two fingers rolling off the ball to the left (Figure 33). This motion generally makes the fastball tail or rise or both. A sidearm pitcher will cut through and

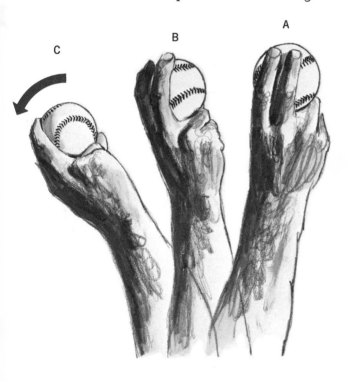

Figure 33. Moving Fastball.
A three-quarters or overhand pitcher makes his fastball move by rolling his fingers to the left as he releases the ball.

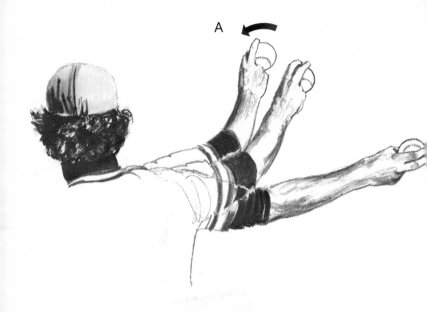

Figure 34. Moving Sidearm Fastball.
To make a sidearm fastball move, cut through
and over the ball as it is released (A).
The ball should either tail in (B) or sink (C).

over the top of the ball (Figure 34) to make it sink. These "artificially" thrown fastballs have the advantage of more movement than a regularly thrown fastball, but a pitcher loses speed when he no longer cuts directly through the heart of the ball.

Most fastballs should be thrown in one of two spots: low and away from a batter, or high and inside (Figure 35). These are the two most difficult fastballs for a batter to hit. To hit a low-and-outside fastball a batter must reach both out and down for the pitch, which, if thrown fast enough, will already be by him. He has only to reach directly outside for a high-outside fastball, which makes it a much easier pitch to hit. The advantage of a high-and-inside fastball is that the closer the pitch gets to a batter's

B

C

eye the greater its speed appears to be. It is an optical illusion, really, but one which invariably throws off a batter's timing. So, these are the ideal spots, and a pitcher should work back and forth between them in setting up a batter.

Whether the fastball goes low and away or up and in is determined by the point at which the ball leaves the pitcher's hand (Figure 36). A right-handed pitcher throwing to a right-handed batter can make the ball go up and in by

Figure 35. Spotting the Fastball.
High and inside or low and away are the two best
targets for the fastball.

releasing the ball soon after it passes his ear. To make that fastball travel low and on the outside corner of the plate the pitcher merely holds onto the ball longer and releases it farther out in front of his head. Knowing when to release the ball is a question of "feel." Feel is not easy to come by and takes a great deal of practice, which is why control is such an elusive element for most pitchers. However, if a pitcher throws with a classically correct motion, his chances for acquiring a high degree of feel are excellent.

Figure 36. Release Points.
A pitcher uses different release points to move his fastball. An early release (A) produces a high, inside pitch to a right-handed batter, a normal release (B) puts the ball across the center of the plate, and a slightly delayed release (C) puts the ball down and outside.

CURVEBALL

The curveball is one of the most difficult pitches to throw correctly. Properly thrown, it is *the* hardest pitch for a batter to hit. The best-breaking curveball is the one which breaks straight down, with little or no right-to-left break. This seems to contradict an earlier statement that a ball moving in two directions—down and right to left—is preferable to a ball moving in only one direction. However, this rule does not apply with a curveball, since, if it is thrown properly, it will spin like a fastball, only in the opposite direction—downward. Approaching the batter, a down-breaking curveball appears to be spinning like a fastball, and the batter, looking down on it, is unable to tell when that ball begins to break. His vantage point—looking down on a sinking object—creates an optical illusion. However, if that same curveball were also breaking from right to left, the batter could pick up that point when the ball begins to break from right to left, tell himself the pitch was a curveball, and adjust his swing accordingly. Another reason it is easier to hit a right-to-left breaking curveball than a straight-down-breaking one is that a batter has almost 36 inches of bat length with which to reach the one breaking horizontally, while he has only about 1 inch of bat width to hit the one that is breaking straight down. Also, the down-breaking curveball is equally effective thrown to either a right-handed or a left-handed batter.

But whatever kind of curveball, the grip remains the same (Figure 37A). The pitcher's first two fingers are tightly together but running parallel to the ball's seams, not bisecting them as with the fastball. The second finger rides alongside of the seam and the first finger presses against the second finger. The pressure points run all along the length of the fingers rather than only at the meaty tips, as with a fastball. The thumb runs parallel to the seam on the underside of the ball (Figure 37B) and exerts pressure

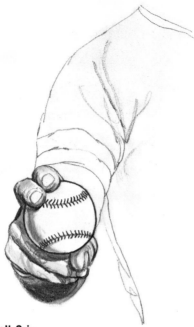

Figure 37. Curveball Grip.
A. The ball is gripped tighter and deeper in the hand than
with the fastball. Notice that fingers are parallel to
and gripping the seams.

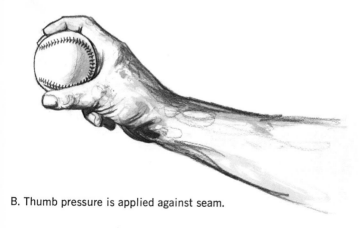

B. Thumb pressure is applied against seam.

against it all along the length of the thumb and not just at the knuckle. And the ball is gripped much tighter than a fastball, with almost no air space between the inside of the palm and the ball. The knuckle of the third finger is also pressed against a seam, so that when the pitcher releases the ball he actually has three sustained pressure points on the seams to give the ball a maximum amount of spin.

To throw a straight down-breaking curveball, a pitcher must throw the ball with an overhand motion. However, until his arm passes alongside of his head, he does nothing different from when he is throwing a fastball; his first two fingers on the baseball are still aimed directly at the plate. Only when the ball passes in front of his head do changes take place which turn an apparent fastball into a curveball. His first two fingers begin to ride up and over the ball while simultaneously turning from right to left (Figure 38). Just before the ball passes above and in front of the pitcher's vision, he yanks his first two fingers down over the side of the ball facing the batter. His wrist continues to rotate forward and down and his forearm is yanked sharply from right to left and down (Figure 39). When the ball is in front of the pitcher's vision and at a level with his cap (his forearm is now bent almost parallel to his vision) his first two fingers should be facing the batter and his thumb facing his vision. At this point the ball spins off his first two fingers, aided by a forward upthrusting motion of his thumb, and heads toward the plate with a severe down-spinning motion. The pitcher's forearm continues passing down across his chest and in toward his left side, following through with his right hand tucked in at his left waist, almost as if the arm were wrapped around a woman's waist while dancing.

Figure 38. Curveball: Arm Motion.
The first two fingers ride up and over the ball (A)
while the arm moves from right to left and simultaneously
is yanked downward (B). The wrist bends
in (C), so that the ball is released up over
the two forward fingers at eye level.

Figure 39. Curveball: Full Motion

B. Only as the arm continues forward
does the yanking motion begin
with the fingers going over the ball.

A. Until the throwing arm passes the head,
the pitching motion is the same
as the fastball.

This sharp yanking motion of both the pitcher's wrist and
his forearm gives the ball its excessive downspin, which
causes the ball to approach the plate and suddenly drop
sharply. To give the pitch its sharpest break, the yanking
motion should occur at a point about 6 inches in front of
and above the pitcher's vision. If a pitcher yanks too soon,
the ball will have a larger, more leisurely break, and just

74

C. During the follow-through the arm continues down and across the body.

D. The arm ends up wrapped around the waist.

roll up to the plate (shown in Figure 43). This rolling type of curveball is an excellent change-of-pace pitch, but it should not be a bread-and-butter curveball. The sooner the pitcher cocks his wrist before reaching the release point, the slower and bigger will be the pitch's break.

If the pitcher finds himself breaking the curveball into the dirt instead of over the plate, the chances are he is not taking a long enough stride. His left foot is coming down too soon, causing him to yank and release early so that the ball breaks before it crosses the plate. To remedy this a pitcher should merely lengthen his stride. Conversely, if the pitch is breaking too high as it crosses the plate, the pitcher's stride is probably too long and he should shorten it by bringing his left foot down sooner.

75

Ideally, all curveballs should break in one general area, over the lower outside corner of the plate. And the ideal curveball should break across the plate as a low strike caught by the catcher almost in the dirt. This pitch is almost impossible for a batter to hit solidly.

Both a three-quarter curveball and a sidearm curveball are thrown exactly as the overhand curveball. However, because the angle of the arm in both cases is moving more right to left than straight down, the ball will have more of a right-to-left break. But in both cases it should also break down more sharply from a three-quarters angle than from a sidearm angle.

A common mistake all pitchers make occurs when the pitcher's fingers and wrist rotate from right to left around the ball rather than up and over the ball (Figure 40). This produces a flat curveball that has no downward break at all, but merely moves from right to left. Sometimes this curveball will even rise slightly into the batter's vision, making it the easiest of all curveballs to hit.

SLIDER

A slider is one of the easiest pitches to throw but one of the most difficult to control, since it must be thrown only to certain spots or it will be exceedingly easy to hit. Pinpoint control is essential. Also, since a slider is a slip pitch thrown with a stiff wrist and a sharp snap of the elbow,

Figure 40.
Curveball: Wrong Rotation.
If the pitcher comes around the ball
instead of over it, his curve will
fail to break, giving the batter
an easy pitch to hit.

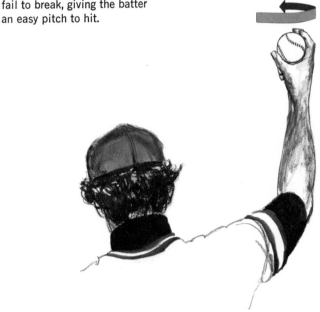

it often produces a sore arm. Therefore, a pitcher working on a slider should quit the moment he feels any pain or stiffness in his elbow. A properly thrown curveball and fastball are nowhere near as dangerous to an arm as a slider.

Now the advantages of a slider. It is an easy pitch, learned in minutes. It is extremely deceptive because it comes in hard, it appears to be a fastball, and at no point can one tell that it is a breaking pitch. Actually it does not break; it is more of a moving fastball than a curveball (Figure 41, A). A curveball can be graphed; that is, one can plot that point in its travels to the plate when it begins to break (Figure 41, B). No such point can be plotted

Figure 41.
The Slider: Batter's View.
A slider appears to be a fastball but moves subtly off the outside corner of the plate (A). A curveball has a distinct break downward as it approaches (B).

Figure 42.
Slider Grip.
A slider is gripped like a curve but deeper
and slightly off center.

with a properly thrown slider. It appears to be heading for
the center of the plate and then, in the midst of his swing,
the batter discovers that his calculations were off, the ball
having moved subtly and deceptively off the outside corner
of the plate. A slider is ideally thrown when a batter is
guessing fastball. As it approaches the heart of the plate,
looking for all the world like a mediocre fastball, the batter
will attack the pitch and will probably either swing wildly
or hit a routine fly or groundball.

79

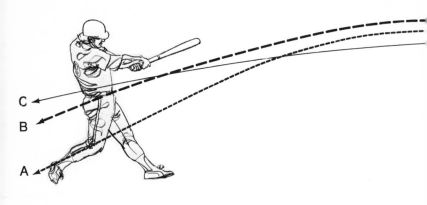

Figure 43. Different Breaking Balls.
A curveball spins away from pitcher,
causing the ball to "break" sharply downward
as it approaches the plate,
crossing below the batter's knees (A).
A slow "hanging" curve (B) fails to break sharply
and has a gentle arc, usually a result
of yanking the ball too soon.
A slider (C) appears not to break at all,
an illusion; it actually breaks much later
and more subtly than a good curveball.

A slider is gripped like a curveball, only the ball is held deeper in the palm and slightly off center, so that more of the white of the ball is exposed between the first finger and thumb (Figure 42). A slider has already become a slider

when the pitcher's hand passes alongside of his head. Unlike a fastball or a curveball, both of which pass the pitcher's head with the first two fingers aiming at the plate, a slider passes the pitcher's head with the first two fingers slightly on top of the ball and aiming toward the outside corner of the plate. The pitcher's wrist is firmly cocked, almost as if he is throwing a football (Figures 44A, 44B, 44C). As the pitcher's arm follows through, at no point does his wrist rotate as with a curveball, or flick forward and down as with a fastball. His wrist must remain perfectly stiff so that his arm continues straight toward the plate with the ball held off center. At the moment of release the ball merely slips out of the pitcher's hand with an off-center, right-to-left, and downward spin. It approaches the plate moving slightly right to left and down, but at no point does it actually begin to break.

Figure 44. The Slider: Arm Motion.
The wrist is cocked and the fingers
are slightly on top of the ball
as the arm passes the head (A).

A

As mentioned before, a slider is an easy pitch to learn to throw, yet is a difficult pitch to control because it must be thrown almost entirely in one spot—low and on the outside corner of the plate to a right-handed batter and waist-high and inside to a left-handed batter. (The reverse is true of a left-handed pitcher.) A slider is the only breaking pitch occasionally thrown waist high, but only to an opposite-handed batter. An inside waist-high slider to a left-handed batter will be hit on the handle of the bat. If the pitch is thrown low and inside, the left-handed batter still has a chance to golf the pitch down the right-field line.

At release (C),
the ball rolls off the hand
with an off-center spin.
The wrist never breaks.

B

C

The wrist must remain stiff
as the arm continues
toward the plate (B).

CHANGE-UP

A change-up is very difficult to throw and control, and yet it can be one of the most deceptive of pitches (Figures 45A, 45B, 45C, 45D). It is held and thrown exactly as a fastball until the ball passes in front of the pitcher's head during his delivery. The moment the arm moves in front of his head, a number of things happen. Instead of the pitcher's wrist moving ahead of his elbow as with a fastball, the reverse occurs. The pitcher's elbow shoots ahead of his

83

Figure 45. The Change-Up.
The change-up motion begins like a fastball (A), but when the arm passes the head, the elbow shoots ahead of the wrist and drops (B).

wrist and is yanked almost straight down. This motion forces the pitcher to merely flip the ball with his forearm and wrist without the benefit of his shoulder and upper-arm strength. Although he is throwing the ball as hard as he can, the ball goes much slower than normal. The batter sees the pitcher's arm moving as fast as with a fastball

C

D

This dissipates much of the built-up power, and the ball is thrown with only the forearm and wrist (C), resulting in a soft, slow pitch (D).

and will adjust his swing accordingly, only to be fooled by the pitch. Generally, a change-up should be thrown very low so that it passes across the plate as a ball or a very low strike. It should never be thrown higher than a batter's knees, or inside.

A change-up is a pitch that should ideally be thrown when a batter is guessing fastball and inclined to swing. Therefore, it is a perfect pitch to throw when the pitcher is behind the batter in count, say, two balls and no strikes, and the batter has the go-ahead sign from his coach. It is the kind of pitch that gets the pitcher out of ticklish situations with one throw, since it is usually weakly hit.

3
Setting Up the Batter

THE CONTEST between the batter and the pitcher hinges upon the pitcher's ability to keep the batter mentally off stride. A pitcher does this by varying the speed and position of his pitches. Some power pitchers can be successful merely by overpowering batters with blazing fastballs and curveballs that fall off a table. But those pitchers are the exception to the rule. The pitcher with more modest "stuff" must rely on cunning and control to outduel the batter.

In general, a pitcher will try to keep the ball low and away from the batter with an occasional high-and-inside pitch thrown for effect. Unless a pitcher has exceptional speed, a high-and-inside fastball should be thrown to force the hitter back from the plate, not necessarily to make him swing at the pitch. No matter how weak a batter is, if he is thrown nothing but a steady diet of low-and-away pitches, sooner or later he'll adjust his swing and hit one of them.

The ratio of fastballs to curveballs to sliders to change-ups a pitcher throws each game should be determined not only by which pitches are generally his best but which pitches are working best for him that day. If a pitcher has an excellent curveball on a certain day, he should not work it to death, but save it for his toughest situations. Neither should a pitcher ever abandon his weakest pitch on a given day; he should try to use it in certain spots to keep a batter off balance—not necessarily to get him to swing at it. Thus a pitcher should "show" a batter his weakest stuff but throw it to a spot, say, off the plate, where a batter can't hit it. A curveball in the dirt reminds the batter that the pitcher possesses such a pitch while still not giving the batter a chance to hit it. It is one more pitch the batter must think about.

No matter whether the batter is a fastball or a curveball hitter, in a crisis situation the pitcher must go with his strength, even if that strength is the batter's. Thus, against Johnny Bench, a fastball hitter, Tom Seaver will go mainly with his fastball. He will have a better chance of retiring Bench with his fastball than Bench will have of hitting it. At best, major-league hitters hit in only three out of ten chances at bat. The percentages are in the pitcher's favor.

If a pitcher discovers a batter's blind spot, a spot where the batter seems incapable of hitting the ball, the pitcher should not work that spot to death. He should save it for ideal situations. Any batter, no matter how weak, who is thrown every pitch to his blind spot will soon learn to hit those pitches. Also, if a batter has a strong spot, a pitcher should not abandon that spot forever. He should wait for an ideal situation and then try to get the batter out with a pitch to his strong spot.

If a batter swings and misses a bad pitch, the pitcher should throw the next pitch in the same spot—only more so. In other words, if a batter swings at a shoulder-level fastball and misses it, the pitcher should throw the next pitch at the batter's eye level. If again the batter swings and misses, the pitcher should throw the next one even higher and see what happens. He may have discovered the batter's blind spot.

When a pitcher is ahead of a batter in count, say two strikes and one ball, he should try to get the batter to swing at a bad pitch off the plate. When, on the other hand, the pitcher is behind the batter, say two balls and no strikes, he will have to throw a strike, and it should be the type of pitch a batter is least expecting. An off-speed pitch—slider, curveball, or change-up—is most effective, since batters generally look for fastballs when they are ahead of the pitchers in count.

The farther ahead of a batter a pitcher is, the more pitches he can waste in setting up his opponent for his "out" pitch. For instance, with two strikes and no balls on a batter, a pitcher may waste two successive high-and-inside fastballs to set up a low-and-outside curveball, or he may throw two low-and-outside curveballs to set up a high-and-inside fastball.

Generally, a free-swinging power hitter like Dave Kingman can be fooled by varying the speed of the pitches. A singles hitter like Pete Rose of the Reds can be gotten out by changing the type of pitches, fastball to slider to curveball. A weak hitter can be gotten out mostly with fastballs and sliders, and should rarely be thrown an off-speed pitch. Usually he's weak because his swing is too slow; he can't get his bat around quick enough on fastballs, but an off-speed pitch is just the kind of slow pitch he can adjust to.

Here is one way a pitcher can set up and dispatch a batter:

1st pitch—curveball low and on the outside corner of the plate for strike one.

2nd pitch—slow curveball low and outside for ball one.

3rd pitch—fastball low and outside for strike two.

4th pitch—fastball high and inside to straighten the batter up, since he is probably, by now, mentally and physically leaning over the plate in anticipation of another outside-corner pitch. Ball two.

5th pitch—with the count 2-and-2, a good fastball low and outside should get the batter. However, if it misses and the count runs to 3-and-2, a pitcher can do the following:

6th pitch—a good breaking ball should fool the batter or a slider on the outside corner of the plate, or a good curveball. Strike three.

Remember, keep the batter guessing. Change speeds and spots continually. Don't ever let the batter set himself in the batter's box with the knowledge of what pitch is coming to what spot. A pitcher who keeps the batter guessing can succeed with only modest ability, while a pitcher who has superior ability but is obvious and predictable will be less successful.

4
Pitching
to Situations

WITH NO ONE ON BASE, the pitcher's first concern is to throw strikes. He will be less accurate in regard to the corners of the plate than he would be with a runner on third base. His objective is to throw the ball over the plate until the batters prove to him that this is not enough, that he must be closer with his control. No matter how feeble a pitcher feels his fastball may be, he should throw it until batters prove they can hit it. In the twilight of his career Robin Roberts, the great Phillies pitcher, once pitched a shutout with a fastball that seemed to creep up to the plate. Yet Roberts believed he could get batters out with that fastball, and he did.

With a runner on first base and one or none out, a pitcher should try to keep his pitches low in the hope that the batter will hit a groundball into a double play. The pitcher should lead this batter off with a straight overhand curve in the hope that he will be swinging on the first pitch. All down-breaking pitches are harder for a batter to hit into the air.

With a runner only on second base, a pitcher can be extra fine with the batter. If he walks him, he will set up the possibility of either a force play at any base or a double play. This is the one circumstance when to walk a batter is almost preferable to giving him anything good to hit at. This is the ideal situation in that the pitcher can now throw his best stuff in the finest spots without worrying about walking the batter.

With a runner on third base and none or one out, the pitcher must try to get the batter out, either on a strikeout or a ground ball. A fly ball to the outfield will score a run as easily as will a base hit.

It is a good idea for the pitcher with runners on base to let the infielders know what pitches he is throwing—a curveball, a fastball, or whatever. There should be some signal to them from either the catcher or the pitcher. This will help them play the hitters.

With runners on base, a pitcher must repeatedly decide what he will do with the ball when and if it is hit back to him—and he must decide this before the pitch, not after it, when it is too late. He should make an automatic habit of this because once he focuses his attention on his pitching, nothing should interfere with his concentration on setting up and dispatching the batter. A pitcher is first of all a pitcher and must devote most of his energies and concentration to each pitch. Everything else is secondary—fielding bunts, throwing to the right base, and so forth.

Also, a pitcher should never alter the pattern of his pitching to satisfy a catcher or infielder. For instance, with a runner on first base who has a good chance of stealing second on the next pitch, a catcher likes to call for fastballs, which get to him quicker and are easier to handle, giving him a better chance to throw out the runner stealing. However, a pitcher's first duty is to retire the batter, and often it will do him no good whatsoever to try to help his catcher.

If he accommodates him, the result is often a hit to the outfield on a fastball the pitcher knew he shouldn't have thrown.

No matter what the situation, a pitcher should never let up physically or mentally, but should always throw his best stuff. If you always throw with your best, most natural motion, control should come naturally. But don't sacrifice your best pitches for control. For instance, with the bases loaded and a 3-and-2 count on the batter, throw your best pitch now, not just a pitch you hope will be a strike. It is better to walk the batter than to throw a mediocre pitch that might be solidly hit. If there is one cardinal rule for a pitcher, it is: Win or lose, make sure you give them your best.